POUR

Pouring Purpose: Inspiring You to Live, Love, and Believe Again

By:

LaTonia Harrell

Believe in yourself and the beauty of new beginnings, for every step you take brings you closer to the life you were meant to live."

~LaTonia Harrell

POUR

Published by LaTonia Harrell

Scripture References
This book includes passages from the following translations:
- King James Version (KJV)
- New Living Translation (NLT)
- New International Version (NIV)

All scripture quotations are used with permission. The translations are copyrighted and are provided for the purpose of enhancing the reader's understanding of the messages conveyed in this work.

Author's Note
This book is written the way God intended for the message to be delivered. It reflects the divine inspiration behind the words and the truths presented.

Author's email- loveandblessings01@gmail.com

ISBN: 979-8-218-98806-7

Copyright Notice
© 2024 LaTonia Harrell. All rights reserved.
This book is a product of the author's original work and guarantees that the contents are original and do not infringe upon the legal rights of any other person or work.

LaTonia Harrell

TABLE OF CONTENETS

1. Positive Affirmations: The power of words and how to use them effectively.

2. Overcoming Fear: Strategies to face and conquer your fears.

3. Resilience: Building mental strength to bounce back from setbacks.

4. Emotional Well-being: Understanding and managing your emotions.

5. Celebrating Small Wins: Recognizing progress to maintain motivation.

6. Finding Your Purpose: Discovering what truly motivates and inspires you.

7. Healing from Unforgiveness: Embracing Brokenness to Find Freedom.

8. Overcoming Rejection: Rebuilding Your Self-Worth after Heartbreaks

   - Discuss strategies for healing from the pain of rejection and rediscovering self-love.

9. Transforming Brokenness into Strength: The Path to Forgiveness and Renewal.

10. Healing Over Betrayal: Reclaiming Trust and Moving Forward.

11. Self-Care: Me Time

12. The Power of Prayer: The Life Line to God

A lot of wisdom, knowledge and encouragement!

POUR

ACKNOWLEGMENT

I want to take a moment to express my heartfelt gratitude to God, who is the head of my life. His grace, mercy, love, and forgiveness have been my guiding light. I am not a perfect woman, but I strive daily to live a life that is pleasing and acceptable unto Him.

I thank God for the God-given assignments He has entrusted to me, for the missions He has set before me, and for the gifts and talents He has graciously bestowed upon me. His continuous pouring into my life allows me to pour into others.

I am especially grateful for the support of my family and friends, whose encouragement has been invaluable on this journey. To all those God-given connections who have, in some form, encouraged me along the way, I thank you.

It is my hope to lead people to Christ, helping them realize that they are not a mistake, that they have a purpose, and that there is nothing too hard for God. May we all embrace our unique paths and trust in His plan for our lives. To Him be all honor and glory forever.

INTRODUTION

In a world often overshadowed by doubt and despair, it's easy to feel lost, unworthy, or disconnected from our true selves. Many of us carry the weight of past hurts, unfulfilled dreams, and the relentless noise of negativity that can suffocate our mind, body and spirit. Yet, within each of us lies an untapped reservoir of potential, restoration, healing and deliverance.

"POUR" is not just a title; it's a call to action. It symbolizes the act of pouring out our fears, pain, and resentment, making room for hope, love, and purpose. This book is a guide for anyone who has ever felt broken, lost, confused or abandoned, urging you to embrace your journey towards healing and fulfillment.

Through heartfelt stories, practical insights, and empowering exercises, I invite you to explore the transformative power of living with intention. Together, we will navigate the complexities of forgiveness, resilience, and self-discovery. Each chapter is designed to inspire you to reclaim your dreams, reconnect with your passions, and believe in the possibility of a brighter tomorrow.

As we embark on this journey together, remember: you are not alone. Every page is infused with encouragement and love, aimed at helping you recognize that your past does not define you. You have the strength to rise, to pour out your heart, and to fill your life with purpose.

Let this be your moment of awakening. It's time to live, love, and believe again.

POSITIVE AFFIRMATIONS

We, having the same spirit of faith, according as it is written: "I believed and therefore have I spoken" — we also believe and therefore speak,

2 Corinthians 4:13. KJV

Affirmations are words used to confirm that something is true about someone or something. When you then say "Positive affirmation", you are ensuring that anything you say about someone, something, or yourself is uplifting and empowering.

They go beyond confessions because it takes conviction to affirm a thing about someone or something. Confession is a declaration made about someone or something. We confess because we know something about someone or something and have affirmed them to be true; otherwise, they'll be mere repetition of words without any power resident in them.

According to the text you read at the beginning of this chapter, the order is stated; believe first, then speak next! Your confession becomes effectual not because you said what was written but because you believed what was written, then it became empowering words to you.

This means that your words are not just words but they are conviction. This is the spirit of faith!! According to faith, we do not see to speak, we speak to see. What enables us to speak is that Spirit resident within us that compels us to know who we are in Christ and to know the riches we have in Christ. Note, this doesn't say the riches we will have in Christ; no, the Spirit empowers us to know the riches we have in Christ.

"To me, though I am the very least of all the saints, this grace was given, to preach to the Gentiles the unsearchable riches of Christ," Ephesians 3:8. KJV

"According as his divine power hath given unto us all things that pertain unto life and godliness, through the knowledge of him that hath called us to glory and virtue: Whereby are given unto us exceeding great and precious promises: that by these ye might be partakers of the divine nature, having escaped the corruption that is in the world through lust." 2 Peter 1:3-4. KJV

"And he said unto them, Unto you it is given to know the mystery of the kingdom of God: but unto them that are without, all these things are done in parables" Mark 4:11 KJV

There are good things in Christ, and nothing can be more true than Jesus Christ himself. Truth is true when it is scripture-compliant. This means that I can superimpose truth on my facts; this is why I need conviction about what is truth before I can confess it or make it my daily affirmation.

In the second Bible reference, we read in the Book of 2 Peter, we read "whereby are given unto us exceeding great and precious promises: that by these ye might be partakers of the divine nature..." It means that you partake in the divine nature of God when you receive and acknowledge these exceeding great and precious promises. Think of the promises of God contained in the scripture, meditate on them, and speak them back to yourself. What comes alive and true is not the nice things you have to say about yourself, it is the nice things Christ says about you that you have to rehearse to yourself and speak them into your atmosphere.

"I'm blessed by the Lord; surely there is an end to affliction."

"I'm a goodly land; I flow with milk and honey, I'm Beulah and Hephzibah."

"The lines are falling for me in pleasant places"

"... He anointed my head with oil, my cup runs over."

These are all examples of exceeding great and precious promises when they become your conviction, your mouth will declare them! Your words carry power when they come from the place of conviction. They become active and sharp:

"For the word of God is quick, powerful, and sharper than any two-edged sword, piercing even to the dividing asunder of soul and spirit, and of the joints and marrow, and is a discerner of the thoughts and intents of the heart." Hebrews 4:12 KJV.

POUR

We know that the words are the word of God, but because you have owned the word, it becomes your word: quick and powerful. "Quick and power-full." When you speak them over your life or circumstances, the effect is great. You can create your reality by the words you speak; you can change the narrative by the words you speak, the effective and potent word of God.

Here, I have taught you how to engage in positive affirmations. I have shown you the difference between confession and affirmation; I told you that your confession may be empty if you do not have a strong conviction about them. I also taught you that what makes your affirmation powerful is that it is backed up by the spirit of faith that compels you to speak what you believe. Oh, I can see you wake up with the understanding that this is the day that the Lord has made; you rejoice, and you are glad in it: by personalizing it, you say, "I rejoice, and I'm glad in it." Listen, this becomes a powerful declaration because you said it from a place of conviction!

You may have debts to pay, you may have projects to carry out, or you may be dealing with a situation that doesn't allow you to say these words. Remember, it is the spirit of faith! The spirit of faith says things that are not as though they are, and through faith, we understand that the worlds were framed by the word of God so that things that are seen were not made of things that do appear. Hebrews 11:3. The creative materials of faith are not tangible but they can substantiate the invincible.

In conclusion,

I want to remind you of the scripture according to Philemon 1:6 "That the communication of thy faith may become effectual by the acknowledging of every good thing which is in you in Christ Jesus." KJV Beloved, there are good things in you in Christ Jesus, they yearn for expression, they yearn for your acknowledgment. You must learn to see them and say them; to easily identify them, you are permitted to say only what you can find in Christ Jesus. Whatever you can't find in Jesus Christ, they should not be found in you, whatever you find in Jesus Christ, acknowledge that they are also found in you.

"I am above only."

"Nothing dies in my hands."

"I have a sound mind."

"I am led by the Spirit of God, I make wise decisions."

"I overcome challenges and challenging times."

"I finish strong and I finish well."

Which other ones can you remember? Before you turn to the next chapter, speak them over your life and the circumstances around you!

OVERCOMING FEAR

"And there we saw the giants, the sons of Anak, which come of the giants: and we were in our own sight as grasshoppers, and so we were in their sight."

Numbers 13:33

One of the things we learned in the previous chapter is that we speak what we believe. Words do not only reflect how we think; they also reflect what formed our mindset, and they reflect our beliefs. In the same way, there is the spirit of faith; there is also the spirit of fear. In the same way, faith can be communicated, fear can also be communicated. In the opening text, we see an example of the communication of fear. Let's see the effect of this communication on the people before we continue.

"And all the congregation lifted their voice, and cried, and the people wept that night." Numbers 14:1.

Fear made the congregation lift their voice, and they cried; they wept that night. The night fear was communicated to them.

Have you ever been so scared to turn the light on even though you know that light could have dispelled the darkness?

This was the situation Israel was once in only because they had the wrong perspective about their situation.

Perception is a great form of exposure and also deliverance. Where there is the wrong perception, there will be the wrong conclusion. Many people are held bound by the wrong perception, and as a result, they create numerous 'what ifs'. One of the miracles God can give to anyone is the miracle of sight beyond eyes. Perception seems to be insight, foresight, and perhaps sight. How do you see yourself? How do you see the situation? How do you see the land, the job, the marriage, the business, the ministry, and other activities you engage in? Some people overestimate what they can achieve in a year and underestimate what they can achieve in a lifetime, and the result is a difference in perception. A man cried out to Jesus Christ, who was passing, "Oh, that I may receive my sight!"

"And Jesus stood, and commanded him to be brought unto him: and when he was come near, he asked him,

Saying, What wilt thou that I shall do unto thee? And he said, Lord, that I may receive my sight." Luke 18:40-41 KJV

Maybe, like this man, you too may need to receive your sight; you may need the right perception about what is happening with you and around you. What breeds fear is a concentration on the wrong things or the right things with a wrong perception. Job had a similar experience; "For the thing which I greatly feared is come upon me, and that which I was afraid of is come unto me." He focused on the wrong things. You focus on the wrong things when you try to control the outcome of everything; your part is to be obedient, but the outcome is God's responsibility. There is such a thing as peace in the storm: this is for those who have obeyed, yet all hell is breaking loose; God guarantees peace! This is not the kind of peace the world gives, this is peace amid chaos. The world's peace is peace after chaos but the peace that beats comprehension is the peace that makes people wonder how you can be so glad even when everything seems to be falling apart. Anxiety is what you feel whenever you are afraid that you may lose everything, that you may lose the marriage, that you may lose your job, that you may lose the house, or that the car may be repossessed. Here's the antidote: "Do not be anxious about anything, but in every situation, by prayer and petition, with thanksgiving, present your requests to God." Philippians 4:6

When you are faced with a daring situation, do not see yourself compared to the situation, see the one who created the world and everything in it. The reason is because greater is he that is in you than he who is in the world. Troubles will come, but Jesus Christ has overcome them on your behalf, so it is not your fight, but it's certainly going to be your victory!

Fear feeds on doubt, and whenever you are in doubt you are simply opening the door for the devil to sow tars on the field of God's promises to you. Fear needs an open door just as faith needs an open door.

While faith is the expectation of a positive outcome, fear is the expectation of a negative outcome only that faith needs a corresponding act of obedience but fear simply needs a corresponding act of doubt to be established.

Most times, as believers, we do not prepare our hearts to be courageous; courage is a dogged contradictory action in the face of fear.

POUR

Most people who moved with God and did great things in the kingdom, people who fulfilled their purpose and aligned to the destiny God has prepared for them did so with fear glaring at them. They knocked fear with a strong conviction!

" For the which cause I also suffer these things: nevertheless I am not ashamed: for I know whom I have believed, and am persuaded that he can keep that which I have committed unto him against that day." 2 Timothy 1:12.

Nothing beats conviction. Conviction, as we have learned, makes you mad. A little David running toward Goliath is absurd, three Hebrew boys willing to be cast into the burning furnace even if God decides not to save them is absurd, an Esther willing to meet King Ahasuerus even without his invitation is absurd, a Gideon willing to go to battle with 300 soldiers against thousands of soldiers is absurd. However, all these people have one thing in common, what is recorded in the verse you just read: they know whom they have believed.

What do you believe?

The Bible lets us know that not everyone will do exploit, but only those who know their God.

You have to know something to be courageous about something, and if what you know is greater than life itself, you will not succumb to fear.

If you refer back to our previous chapter, you'll understand that your positive affirmations are not mere words of faith, they are life-giving words that empower you to act boldly in the face of a difficult situation.

At the beginning of this chapter, I told you that there is the spirit of faith just as there is the spirit of fear. Fear is overcome by light, perfect enlightenment! If you know that you will come out stronger, bigger, and better, will you be afraid?

"For God hath not given us the spirit of fear; but of power, and love, and a sound mind." 2 Timothy 1: 7

You have a sound mind

You have a sound perception

You have a sound understanding. Face your fears with boldness, knowing that before the battle started, you had already won.

POUR

Pouring Purpose: Inspiring You to Live, Love, and Believe Again

LaTonia Harrell

RESILIENCE

"And hearing the multitude pass by, he asked what it meant.

And they told him, that Jesus of Nazareth passeth by.

And he cried, saying, Jesus, thou Son of David, have mercy on me.

And they which went before rebuked him, that he should hold his peace: but he cried so much the more, Thou Son of David, have mercy on me." Luke 18:36-39. KJV

Sometimes God opens doors for you through your determination. In the journey of life, some good things happen to those who have shown how badly they want a thing. So many people along the way quit, but a few dared to keep going until they reached their destination, and a few dared to keep showing up until they got a breakthrough. A lot of the miracles we find in scripture exemplify men and women who have resolved in their hearts that though they suffer infirmity, they won't suffer mental bondage. They believe they can.

Beginning with our text, we will outline a few lessons we can glean from some of the attitudes of people Jesus Christ encountered as he went about doing good and healing all who were oppressed by the devil.

1. The Blind Man:

Though he was blind, he could hear and he can speak; he ensured that a dysfunction in one area of his life didn't override other areas in his life that are functional. How many times have we allowed something in our lives that is not working yet to halt other areas of our lives that are gainfully working?

Think of what his situation could have been if he never took advantage of the fact that he could hear and speak, or what could have been his fate if he was bitter about losing his sight. Rather, as soon as he heard that it was Jesus of Nazareth who was passing by, he shouted for help: "Jesus,

POUR

thou Son of David have mercy on me!" You would think that the people obstacles he was about to face shouting for help would stop him because they tried to quiet him from shouting but he was determined to receive his sight, so he shouted all the more!

He broke through the mental conditioning the people tried to limit him to that could have made him accept his dysfunction as his fate, but he knew what possibilities lay ahead of him, so he screamed until he got the attention of Jesus Christ of Nazareth. If he allowed the people to shut him up, he would have probably never received his sight. If you allow the economy to shut you up, you probably may not see your son again; if you allow what people will say about you to stop you from taking baby steps, you probably may not be free from debts again. Again, in the story, we see that those who shut him up are those who have gone ahead of him; experience, they say, is the best teacher, but I say it is one of the best teachers. Sometimes experience can be a liability even though it can be verified to have truly happened. Some people's experience is just what it is, "their experiences" because yours can be different. They knocked, but the door wasn't opened to them. This does not mean that if you knock, the door will not be opened to you, even if they are sharing with you from experience. Maybe if they had "knocked the more" the door might as well be opened for them. Don't allow people's experiences to lock you in a vault of incapacitation. You must rise to the occasion and use your voice to shout out, and your ears to hear what opportunities you can harness if you are determined to receive your sight.

2. The Paralyzed Man.

"And when they could not find by what way they might bring him in because of the multitude, they went upon the housetop, and let him down through the tiling with his couch into the midst before Jesus.

And when he saw their faith, he said unto him, Man, thy sins are forgiven thee." Luke 5:19-20

The record had it that Jesus was teaching at a certain location, and, because of the multitude of people, could not get to where Jesus was. A few friends had carried their paralyzed friend to that crusade hoping that Jesus would heal him. To them, it wasn't a question of whether Jesus would heal him; they must have thought out that as long as they could put their friend in front of Jesus Christ, their friend would walk again. It is important the kind of people you have around you and what kind of sacrifices they are willing to make to help you get back on your feet. Similar to the story of the blind man, Jesus halted when he heard the man's plea; he also stopped teaching when he saw their faith. The miracles both of them got were great, but also great was their resilience.

Resilience doesn't come into play until there is an obstacle or many obstacles. How bad do you want it?

Those friends are determined to see that their friend gets back to his feet. The blind man is determined to receive his sight. Are you determined about anything? Can you be determined to be a good father? Can you be determined to get your master's degree? Can you be determined to quit smoking? It appears that faith is a fight; this is why it is called the good fight of faith. You will fight through obstacles with resilience and dedication.

As long as you are not defeated mentally, as long as you are not overwhelmed by what you have to go through to get your breakthrough, there is still a good chance that your story will change for the better.

The last story or example I would like to share with you is a popular one, the story of the Woman with the issue of blood.

3. The Woman with no name:

Have you been through anything to the point that to identify you they had to rename you after the situation you were dealing with? In this case, the woman is identified as 'the woman with the issue of blood'. For twelve years, she had been dealing with this disease (about from the time Jairus' daughter was born, up until when they met Jesus for their miracles). She was ostracized, incarcerated, and victimized, yet she had faith: Faith will not respond to a situation where there is no resilience. Some prayers didn't get answered because those who started praying did not add resilience to their quest for a solution. The man who sat at the pool of Bethesda for 38 years was resilient, only that he admitted to not having a man. He says while I am making an effort, another goes into the pool before me; those who have men. Whether it is a situation that has lingered 38 years, 12 years, or 3 months, it takes resilience to push boundaries and set a new record.

"And, behold, a woman, which was diseased with an issue of blood twelve years, came behind him, and touched the hem of his garment: For she said within herself, If I may but touch his garment, I shall be whole." Mark 9:20-21.

What have you been saying within yourself? Has it been the reason you are still getting knocked down?

POUR

Have you been listening to people's experiences that you get scared about your fate? Or have you told yourself "I'll never be whole again."?

I have good news for you,

You can have a great comeback if you choose not to quit. After 38 years, the man walked again; after raising his voice against all odds, the blind man received his sight, and after 12 years, the woman was made whole. What did they have in common? They still believed that they could be better. As long as you are still here, you can come out of anything victorious if you don't quit!

I'm asking you again, how badly do you want it?

Recalibrate your mind, and tell yourself you are not going to stay down; you will get back in the game bigger, stronger, and better. Rise, champion!

LaTonia Harrell

EMOTIONAL WELL- BEING

"Beloved, I wish above all things that thou mayest prosper and be in health, even as thy soul prospereth." 3 John 1:2

You can indeed be a believer and yet experience depression; this is not to say that you are not in Christ, but such a thing is possible only because one neglected his or her emotional well-being.

When some people read through that verse in the Third John, they do not meditate on it to practically understand what it means. They only assume that it is speaking about prospering as a believer. The text acknowledges that there is a lack of prosperity and health in other areas of people's lives when compared to the prosperity of their souls. So John uses the words "even as". Meaning, that he would love them to experience prosperity and health in other areas of their lives even as they are experiencing the prosperity and health of their soul.

The prosperity of the soul becomes the Hallmark of the will of God when you are also emotionally healthy and prospering. The goal is not to build one apart from the other but to build them all up together. As your soul is prospering, your emotional health, Spiritual health, physical health, and financial health are all prospering. This is what John wishes above all things, and by extension, this is the absolute will of God for you to prosper and be in health physically, socially, economically, spiritually, mentally, and emotionally.

Man is a tripartite being; man is body, soul, and spirit. Man is not spirit alone, man is not body alone, and man is not soul alone. The three whole compositions make up the total man.

In Bible class, we teach about the natural, carnal, and spiritual man. Where the natural man is a description of anyone who has not received the life of Christ, the carnal man is the man who has received the life of Christ but is still carnally minded, while the spiritual man is the man who has received cry's but is directed and instructed through the leadership of the Holy Spirit. God intends for every believer to be led by the Spirit of God in his spirit. The maturity of the sons of God means that they have learned how to superimpose the will of God over their will and emotions. This doesn't mean that they have neglected their emotions; it means that they bring their emotions to be subject or submitted to the will of God.

POUR

Here's the balance and that's where we are going: Joy is a fruit of the Spirit; though Joy is resident in your spirit, it is expressed through your emotion. When you are cheerful, jovial, and full of life, it is expressed through your emotions. Also, when you are victimized, abused, and discriminated against, it will be expressed through your emotions. While Joy is the will of God, abuse is not the will of God. When someone gifts you with your dream car, you will become happy even moments after you were sad that you have just missed an appointment. This happens because you have a soul where your emotions are resident and in most cases, your emotions are determined by what is happening around you. This also means that you can control what is happening around you and how you respond to what is happening around you that you cannot control.

Your emotional health and well-being are the will of God. This means you must prioritize your peace, your sanity, and your wholeness by the will of God. God did not put anyone in situations where they were abused, victimized, and dehumanized. Wherever you find abuse, victimization, and dehumanization, there is a dysfunction. Things like depression are the effects of the roots of bitterness, pain, and certain emotional disorders. You don't deal with depression at the level it appears, you deal with it at the root level by understanding what has caused the pain the soul is feeling such that it has endured pain as a culture. However, some persons are depressed from setting unrealistic expectations for themselves while others are thoroughly being abused. Where abuse is the case, depression is an indication that the soul knows that it deserves better. While some people were not taught to take their emotions seriously, others just see their emotions as an open book; anyone can write on it and make any alterations they want to but by this lesson in this book, you will learn how to be emotionally stable and healthy.

If it is true that God planted emotions in us for his glory, as a part of our whole being, it means that he is also interested in how we feel about anything and everything. This is why the Holy Spirit is primarily given to us as a helper and a comforter. I want you to settle it in your heart that God cares about how you feel about your marriage, your job, your life, your husband, your government, your wife, your team, your children, your boss, and everyone connected to you. However, in his wisdom, he has set principles to guide you so that you can have the results he desires for you; he has also set what I like to call rules of engagement that enable you to get standardized results when dealing with things that play a role in your emotional development. There are things you allow in your life that dampen your emotions, and there are things you allow in your life that promote your emotional health.

Further in this lesson, I'll show you things you need to standardize in your life to keep you emotionally balanced and healthy.

HOW TO STAY EMOTIONALLY HEALTHY

1. STANDARDIZE YOUR LIFE:

First things first, you need to culture your life through a standard. Not everything is meant for you and you are not created to fit everything and everyone. Control what comes in and out of your life. Regulate who walks in and out of your life; don't leave it to chance or happenstance. You can live a life by design; you can be happy, and you can be at peace with God, yourself, and others. It begins with setting the standard of what your life deserves especially according to the word of God. When your life has been standardized; your principles will be set, your goals will be set, your circle will be defined, your vision will be clearer, and your time will be strategically put to use. Understand that not all good things are right for you and not all the right things are good for you. Some come into your life as discipline required for the next level and phase of your life, and they may not feel good, but they are necessary ladders for your elevation. When your life is standardized, your results will be standardized.

You will become branded and certain possibilities can come to mind whenever your name is mentioned.

You are happier and healthier when you sense that you are living your life by design.

2. DEFINE WHAT IS IMPORTANT IN YOUR LIFE.

Your ability to define what is important in your life will keep you in check and enable you to stay secure regardless of whatever urgency comes knocking at your door. In a bid to make other people happy or to be validated by others, some people have failed to set up boundaries in their lives. Boundaries help to ensure that you are unavailable for what is not important in your life no matter how urgent it is. What determines what is important in your life is your purpose fulfillment. If it doesn't work out to fulfill God's purpose in your life, it is not important. Whatever you do that is not tied to your purpose will eventually leave you feeling depleted. Emotional stress comes from doing so much without being fulfilled. Fulfillment is like grease to your elbows, it helps to renew your strength and impact.

POUR

I beg to bring to your notice that even some good things are part of the distractions contributing to some people's stress levels because, at the end of the day, when the work, the feelings, and the profit are put on the scale of fulfillment, you discover that it has no weight.

If you start now to reprioritize your activities and pursue only what is purposeful you will notice a tremendous amount of peace and security in your life. That in itself is life!

3. ENDURE WHAT MAKES YOU BETTER.

I will carefully make this point clear because a lot of persons have misunderstood it completely so much so that they endure unnecessary pain calling it process. As I stated earlier, what is profitable, in the end, is only what is connected to your purpose. Even God is committed to making all things work together for the good of those who love him and are called according to PURPOSE. We shall look deeper into the subject of purpose later in this book. When you endure what is not meant for you, it is called self-inflicted wounds. You took it because you don't know what is meant for you and what isn't.

Jesus Christ suffered purposefully; he knew that suffering was more rewarding than growing old with his grandchildren in the streets of Bethlehem. So he called Judas friend and called Peter Satan. Until you can tell the difference between good and right, you may not be definite or bold enough to call certain things off. The devil, most times, doesn't fight you with bad or evil; he accomplishes more with good because he knows if you are busy doing good things instead of the right things, you will have no time to do the right things, which is where the rewards are.

Suffering for being despitefully used can be the right thing, but when you are sexually abused it is not right or good for you. If you marry wrong, you may endure emotional disconnect as the price to pay for not marrying right but not at the expense of jeopardizing the rest of your life. The rest of your life is more important to God than your mistakes of the past.

So, what you should endure is only what makes you better, not what makes you worse or what drains you. I know you know that some painful things are gainful but not all painful things are gainful. You need to discern the will of God in a situation by praying for his will to be done, renewing your mind, and understanding his purpose.

4. DISCERN YOUR WORTH.

"For I say, through the grace given unto me, to every man that is among you, not to think of himself more highly than he ought to think, but to think soberly, according as God hath dealt to every man the measure of faith." Romans 12:3

Your ability to discern your worth keeps you from a need to impress; it keeps you from getting hurt when people don't discern your worth, either. Why do you need to discern your worth?

You need to do so because people will only treat you how you show them to treat you by what you allow and what you don't allow in your life. If you are comfortable when people arrive at your meetings late, they'll have no respect for your time. Whatever you allow to happen to you, especially if you can regulate it, tells people what your value system is about. Until you can properly discern your worth according to the Grace that was given to you, you will not correctly respond to things happening around you or within you.

People learn more about you by what you tolerate and what you support or stand against. All of them put together are a reflection of your self-worth. The text highlighted above shows you how God wants you to project your importance, gracefully!

So far, we have seen four factors that contribute meaningfully to upholding your emotional development and health. May I remind you again that God cares about how you feel, he cares about what you feel. He is willing to help you heal and measure up in areas you truly want to feel alive.

In other chapters of this book, you will learn more about some of the points you need more clarity on as I perceived that you may have a few questions that you want answers for. This book is intentionally written to move you up and forward and transform your life by renewing your mind.

Cheers to a more fulfilling life!

POUR

CELEBRATING SMALL WINS

"Though thy beginning was small, yet thy latter end should greatly increase." Job 8:7

Think about this for a moment if you will. Jesus Christ, the Savior of the world, could have stepped into the earth as a man, grown in stature and wisdom. He could have even chosen to appear in the Earth and Glory, but he rather chose to come in as a baby. This is what he wants you to know: he is not intimidated by your small wins, and he is not ashamed of your little efforts; he started small on the redemption project. If God is not insecure about how little you started or you have little, why should you be insecure about starting small? In fact, throughout history, I discovered that God's mighty works were done with small things. Do we talk about the little flask of oil that Elijah prayed on or the five loaves of bread and the two fishes Jesus multiplied, or the metaphor Jesus used to express faith; saying if you have faith even as small as a mustard seed, you can move mountains, or the "except a corn of wheat falls to the ground it remains alone..."?

All of them speak about small things and just so you know, God was involved in all of them. We can go on and on, no wonder Job assured himself that though his beginning was small, his latter end shall be great. Great things start small, sometimes they start perhaps insignificant and you would understand why there is the instruction that you should not despise the days of little beginning.

" Do not despise these small beginnings, for the LORD rejoices to see the work begin, to see the plumb line in Zerubbabel's hand." (The seven lamps represent the eyes of the LORD that search all around the world.)" Zechariah 4:10 NLT

Do you mean the Lord rejoices to see the work begin?

Let me make it personal for you: the Lord rejoices to see that you start your project no matter how little it is or what you can afford; he wants you to understand that it is better to grow than to jump up. We live in a quick-fist and very competitive world where everyone is making an effort to outdo others, most times at the expense of real growth or establishment. What makes it difficult for a tree to be uprooted is that the roots have been established; until your roots have been established, it is easy to be uprooted. Many businesses, companies, marriages, careers, relationships, or parenting have not been established yet it has gone through a quick growth because people love competition more than they love consolidation. Growth takes time, establishment takes time, and these things happen only to materials that are willing to start small and materials that are willing to acknowledge their small, consistent efforts. How nice it is to know that God loves to see that you have started; instead of waiting for big opportunities, why not start with the small opportunities around you and grow into the big ones that have been set out for you on the other level? But, start!

Many people give excuses for not starting because they don't want to start small, they want to impress people, and they want people to see them as "big and established." Instead of faking it why not patiently work it out?

I know that sometimes it is what is obtainable in a person's environment that influences them; I want you to know that you are different. You don't have to go by what is trending, putting yourself under unnecessary pressures just to fit in, and ending up ungrateful because you don't have or have not achieved as much as the other person you saw has achieved. As long as you are working on purpose and obedient to God's voice, you are right on time and doing great at the pace you should.

My emphasis in this chapter is that you should celebrate your small wins. You may not be where you want to be, but at least you have started and you started on the right foundation following the right principles. Your small wins do not intimidate God; he is pleased with you, so you have to be pleased with yourself and proud of what you have going on. One of the great ways you can be grateful is by acknowledging the little progress you have made. It takes little drops of water to make a mighty ocean: growth can be managed when you start small. A seed has potential fruits in it, but to harvest the fruits from the seed, you must plant the seed, the seed has to germinate, the plant has to grow and the fruits have to mature before you can harvest them. This is the process that growing enables you to participate in, what many people do not know is that they are more established when they are planted than when they are simply positioned.

"Those that be planted in the house of the LORD shall flourish in the courts of our God." Psalm 92:13 KJV.

Faithfulness is not a reward; it is the principle for increase. You cannot increase in areas you have not been faithful to. The reason is that faithfulness is cultivated through stewardship. The principle of growth acknowledges and honors stewardship. If you are a good manager of what is seemingly insignificant, better will be added to you. If you are faithful with little, more will be added to you; the discipline it took to manage small things can be trusted when you have big things because ultimately, you need discipline to grow bigger. I am talking about growth more in

POUR

this chapter because growth doesn't happen overnight. For emphasis, GROWTH DOESN'T HAPPEN OVERNIGHT. Growth happens over time!

If you have a hard time celebrating your small wins, you will be easily discouraged. Many people have quit from good because they want better, and some others have quit from better because they want the best; if only they knew that it gets better little by little over time and not overnight.

Patience is one of the virtues that gives you an advantage if you want to grow an evergreen tree whose leaves shall not wither and whose fruits are good in season and out of season, you cannot underestimate the impact of patience in your growth process. God knows that if you start small, you will certainly grow this is why he sent me to encourage you that your small wins are necessary ladders for your big wins. You are an adult now but it took years for you to eventually become an adult. You would be thankful for your formative age because if you didn't survive those early years you probably wouldn't have been alive to read this book. This means that while we were growing little by little, we were making progress and we were getting better. Again, I want to tell you that those small wins are foundations for your greater impact or influence; you need to honor and preserve it.

Three points you must never forget:

1. Starting small doesn't mean you are small.

2. Your growth is trusted when your journey can prove that you went through the process little by little.

3. No matter how fast you can run if you jump the gun, you will be disqualified.

Great people start small and grow big; the destiny of a seed is to become a tree. Only people who don't know their potential get intimidated by small progress.

In the journey of your destiny, you only need to contend with time: what you call speed is taking advantage of time to achieve more. You don't need speed if you are not yet established, it will destroy you. This is why competing with others in destiny is not wise. You have your lane; your commitment is to run the race that is set before you with perseverance; you run to finish well, not first.

God is a wise master builder; he gives you what you need at the stage you are while he builds your capacity for more. Your small wins may not make you well but they make you better, the little job may not afford to buy you a nice house but it can afford to pay your rent, the opportunities you have may not afford you luxury, but it can afford you a decent meal, keeping you alive while you grow in your stewardship to access more and maturity to influence more.

Before we get to the next chapter, let me dazzle you with what God did with the Israelites on their first days of arrival to the promised land of Canaan:

"Behold, I send an Angel before thee, to keep thee in the way, and to bring thee into the place which I have prepared. Beware of him, and obey his voice, provoke him not; for he will not pardon your transgressions: for my name is in him.

But if thou shalt indeed obey his voice, and do all that I speak; then I will be an enemy unto thine enemies, and an adversary unto thine adversaries. For mine Angel shall go before thee, and bring thee in unto the Amorites, and the Hittites, and the Perizzites, and the Canaanites, and the Hivites, and the Jebusites: and I will cut them off. Thou shalt not bow down to their gods, nor serve them, nor do after their works: but thou shalt utterly overthrow them, and quite break down their images.

And ye shall serve the LORD your God, and he shall bless thy bread, and thy water, and I will take sickness away from the midst of thee.

There shall nothing cast their young, nor be barren, in thy land: the number of thy days I will fulfill.

I will send my fear before thee and will destroy all the people to whom thou shalt come, and I will make all thine enemies turn their backs unto thee.

And I will send hornets before thee, which shall drive out the Hivite, the Canaanite, and the Hittite, from before thee.

I will not drive them out from before thee in one year; lest the land become desolate, and the beast of the field multiply against thee.

By little and little, I will drive them out from before thee until thou be increased and inherit the land." Exodus 23: 20-30.

The last two verses are eye-openers that God did not just take the Israelites into their promised land and hand them the keys, chasing out every occupant in the land immediately after they arrived. No, he said he would not achieve all that in one year; this means that even though he could do that, he chose not to do that in a year because he also wanted the capacity of Israel to increase so that they could manage what he was giving to them. Instead, he will drive the occupants out of the land little by little and, at the same time, increase the capacity and influence of his people, Israel, little by little.

POUR

Friend, as far as you are making even small progress, God is happy with you. Don't beat yourself up thinking that because you are not where you want to be yet you have not left where you used to be. I emphasized growth so that you can see that while you are making little progress; your growth is being established. Therefore, it is wise to celebrate your small wins; counting your blessings and naming them one after the other.

I see you increasing greatly in capacity to be and do more.

FINDING YOUR PURPOSE

Life is meant to be lived with meaning. When you have found the meaning of your life, you will understand why you are gifted in the way that you are gifted and why you are equipped differently. God's Agenda in the earth is his purpose on Earth, but it is carried out by man in the earth. This means you are created on purpose for a purpose. You are not just born into the world by the will of man, even though you are born, you had to be born to begin your assignment in the earth.

"Before I formed thee in the belly I knew thee, and before thou camest forth out of the womb, I sanctified thee, and I ordained thee a prophet unto the nations." Jeremiah 1:5.

God speaking to Jeremiah lets him know that He was born because there is a mandate upon his life that he was born for and that he is predestined to fulfill. If this is true for Jeremiah, it is also true for you and for everyone that is on the earth. Jesus Christ was born to the family of Joseph and Mary but we know he came specially to fulfill the requirements of redemption.

"Then said I, Lo, I come (in the volume of the book it is written of me,) to do thy will, O God." Hebrews 10:7.

There are things written concerning you to be fulfilled in time; these things were written before you were born, and when the time came, you were born.

"For we are his workmanship, created in Christ Jesus unto good works, which God hath before ordained that we should walk in them." Ephesians 2:10.

There are great things written concerning you, you are born to fulfill the purposes of God and on time. Your life becomes rewarding when it is lived to accomplish the purposes of God, remember that God had ordained certain good works that we are to walk in them. They are the things that give meaning to your life and your life in Christ. Your success in life is not tied to random attainment; it is tied to doing the work of your purpose and finishing it. I want it to sink into your heart that you are important to God; you are not a love child; you are called out based on the timing of your assignment; this is why you were born in the time you were. You arrived on Earth, your primary place of assignment, the day you were born. God wants certain possibilities on earth, and he created people (you and I) for certain purposes, knowing that when the time comes for its fulfillment, he will cause a man and a woman to meet so that you can be born. All these things happen in time, and this is why, to fulfill your purpose, you must be familiar with your time and understand it to know what you should be doing and how you should be doing it. Let's go a little deeper.

A lot of people are ambitious but are not purposeful; they want to be successful but they don't want to be purposeful. However, if you can gain dominion over time such that you find your purpose early and define your success from fulfilling your purpose, you will enjoy a life of purpose. In discovering your purpose, you need time and discipline.

TIME AND PURPOSE

Discovering your purpose takes time,

Becoming purposeful takes time,

Becoming focused takes time,

But to find and set the use of time, you have to find purpose first!

I'm a living example of what I teach (Purpose).

I don't do anything outside my purpose; this means I wake up every day taking a step toward my purpose.

As I stated earlier, success is not some random attainment; it must be defined and have its roots in your purpose. Therefore, we must be careful how we define and implement the principles of "becoming" successful.

How do you know you are successful?

The compass for such assurance is within you, not in the news or the trends.

A lot of people are working hard to be successful; of course, you can be successful at doing anything if you follow the principles that make for success, for instance, going to school and graduating with good grades.

Consider these, however, that if you are not properly informed, you can spend time studying and excelling at a course that has entirely nothing to do with your purpose. This means before you start making permanent decisions ensure you are clear on what your purpose is. Don't just be successful; be fulfilled at the attainment of all levels of success.

This is what purpose does for you.

Outside purpose, it is possible for one to attain an enviable height and yet be depressed; this sort of depression is painful because everyone looks at you and wishes they had your life, but deep down, you know you have not lived your life ever, not even once.

"But No knowledge is a waste," you say,

I get it, but no time should be wasted. The real asset here is time not what you used it for.

The value of time is measured by your profit according to the tenets of your purpose not solely by the reward you get for success.

"Are you saying success and purpose fulfillment are not the same things?"

They are not the same things. Purpose gives meaning to success; where there is success without purpose, time is stolen. So when purpose arrived, there was no time available.

Wherever purpose and time meet, they produce fulfillment. The reward of time is purpose. It means that you spent it doing the most important thing: living your purpose.

This also means that if you are SUCCESSFUL doing the wrong thing, you are WASTING your time.

POUR

Without purpose, time is without value. This means that the value of time is enjoyed where purpose is achieved.

Many successful people don't know Jack about their purpose (they try to compensate themselves by doing good work). Faithfulness is not about doing good things; it is about doing purposeful things. Are you serving your purpose or are you just being successful at wasting your own time? I see all those gifts, awards, and affluence, but did they come because you have scratched the depths of your purpose?

I would have told you more about your calling and your purpose. Your calling is not your purpose!

"But I have a calling to sing",

"For me, it is to write"

"Over here, mine is to preach"

I acknowledge all your gifts, but these are tools for your Purpose. They are not your calling!

Jesus was a preacher; he could have sung a few songs, too, if he wanted, but none of that was his calling. His purpose was to save the lost. Even the miracles he performed were not his calling. They are gifts and tools to enable him to fulfill his purpose and assignment.

His purpose was to redeem humanity back to a place of relationship with the Father.

His destiny was to die ON THE CROSS.

He was born to die so that through his death, many can be brought to life.

If he died any other way, HIS PURPOSE OF DYING would have been in vain. If he lived long HIS PURPOSE OF LIVING WOULD HAVE BEEN IN VAIN. If he performed miracles and refused to die, saying he had a calling to perform miracles, his TIME on earth would have been a WASTE.

So, your calling is not your purpose rather, your purpose is your calling!

That very one thing that everything you are or have made you become, first for the kingdom and then for humanity.

If you sing, preach, dance, govern, or design without a sense of purpose, you are making your calling your purpose instead of making your purpose your calling. Your gifts enable you, they do not become! They enable you to become!!!! So, in the blueprint of your purpose, there is time to discover yourself, sharpen your gifts, serve them to fine-tune them, gain mastery, and define them, and then the time to be deployed to the field. All this time is allotted, and the only time you see God conforming all things to work for you is because you are right in and on your Purpose.

So, the mistakes, the people, the movements, disappointment, though it was not his plan, he can use it to fulfill his plan because you have said yes to your assignment.

Your purpose is usually in things you love to do to improve the lives of others which are keen about bringing Glory to God. Your gifts, talents, and abilities prophesy about your purpose. When you realize why you are sent to Earth, you'll understand why your gifts were given to you. Suddenly, everything begins to add up: you notice that your gifts and talents are empowering you to do what you should do in the place of your assignment. You will discover that your compassion, your disappointment about certain things, and your will to make a difference in certain areas are all connected to your purpose.

In the real sense, we don't find our purpose, our purpose finds us. What consistent, strategic, and kingdom-come prayers do is that it is like a force that pushes you like you don't know where you are going, or what you are doing, it pushes you to bring you to that place of your assignment, where your eyes can be enlightened then you can know,

"This is why I am created, I am born for this!"

It takes absolute dependence on God to be discovered by your purpose. Detours are God's strategy to bring you to that place where you'll be effective for him.

But first, you must surrender yourself to a life of meaning and commit yourself to the discipline of being guided by the word of God until the Spirit of God woos you into your ordained place.

Immediately you get there, you will know that that is the place God has ordained for you.

Remember, it takes time to discover your purpose, it takes time to train for your assignment, and it takes time to gain mastery. I'll say you start now by volunteering in the areas of your gifting

POUR

while you pray that God shows you your purpose. Get under methodic mentorship and serve under a mentor and you'll have a better advantage over time.

I'm rooting for you!

LaTonia Harrell

HEALING FROM UNFORGIVENESS

True Healing, whether it is emotional, spiritual, or physical, doesn't have to make you numb. Getting hurt without feeling pain will make you bleed to death. True Healing gives you a fresh start... it is a new 'bud', true healing is refreshing. Hurting from the situation afresh when you remember the incident is a sign that you are still struggling to let go or forgive. My concern, however, is becoming numb.

HAVE YOU BECOME NUMB?

In the midst of all that we all have to bear and go through, it is important to note that in areas of our lives where we are hurting, we need to heal. The trick of the enemy is to make you think that if you keep getting hurt over and again in the same spot, there is no need to get healed; instead, to save yourself the stress of going through the same process again and again, it is easier and better to go numb. Sadly, a lot of people have gone numb and are just alive with no sense of feelings anymore. I thought to reach out to those special ones again. Kindly consider this;

As usual, when I get to do some chores in the house, I receive great insights, so as I meditate on them, the Holy Spirit broods on them and gives me a deeper understanding of such a supply of insight. Just this morning, as I was meditating in the place of my "chores," boom! The shaft of wisdom collided with my mentality to birth what I am about to share with you now.

For emphasis, generally being numb means not being able to respond to feelings normally. Whenever a part of your body is numb, it is unable to feel anything, for example, because you are very cold. Also, you can feel numb in a part of your body because blood has not (does not flow) been able to flow in those areas. I'll need you to follow me closely, and honestly, as I bring forth this timely teaching and message to you; I'm concerned that there are areas in your life that need warmth and need blood.

POUR

From my definition of what it means to be numb and some examples of what causes numbness, I will use them as tools and case studies to bring you some sound insights that I believe will transform you and position you for the next moments and seasons of your life. Experience is always responsible for numbness and I look at it in this light: Someone who is exposed to cold will certainly experience such cold and that results in the numbness of a part of the body, so also with the veins and arteries in our bodies that aid the circulation of blood, if for any reason the vein encounters any obstruction that hinders the necessary supply of blood to parts of the body, such experience will result to the numbness of that part of the body that is "patched". Let's narrow it down to real life, and this is where you benefit even better. Some experiences in your life have either made you go cold or hindered blood from flowing in you. I'll therefore use this opportunity to speak to you as I share with two categories of people. Others can come up in the subsequent chapters as the case may be. They are namely,

THE NO-BLOOD PEOPLE and THE COLD PEOPLE.

Remember that this is the two outstanding cause of numbness in people's lives and maybe, right now in your life.

THE NO-BLOOD PEOPLE:

If you belong to this category, you must have experienced so much hurt that caused you great pain over and over again. You've been through a very grave situation that made you bleed so much that you lost a huge amount of blood. People you trusted, you gave your heart to, relationships you invested your all in, or someone who betrayed you or victimized you has caused you so much blood. You bled until there was nothing like blood in your heart or for your heart, and this experience has left you with the lack of blood and, of course, the NUMBNESS you now feel. Instead of letting go, you chose to go numb. You've said to hell with love, you've resolved not to help anyone again, you've resolved not to trust anyone again, you've resolved not to give your best anymore because you lost Your BLOOD while you were doing what you felt was right, but these experiences have created a deep, a very deep cut in your body that isn't healing as fast as you wish, or maybe it isn't healing because you have given up on being healed, so now you just gave in to being numb.

What you didn't know was that the day you accepted to go numb because you lost blood was the day you gave up being alive. Blood is one of the essential features in the body that makes you alive. When you said I don't need any more blood (which could mean Love, a relationship, trusting someone else, going back to school, raising another child, supporting another upcoming star, forgiving your wife again, forgiving your husband, or yourself and so on, you know what made you bleed), you gave up the opportunity to live again. No wonder you don't feel anything anymore. You don't care anymore; it's not your concern anymore; oh dear, how you gave up being alive because of past hurts. Now you hide behind your mask which is your job, your choir, your blog, your career, or 'ministry' knowing fully that you are "dead" to the vibes you naturally should have responded to. You can't show your real self because blood doesn't even flow in you anymore... you need a transfusion.

Whew! I am calling you out of those dead places of the past and of memories to allow blood to flow in you again. The blood of Jesus is still much available! You need to let dead things go, and like Lazarus, step out of the tomb where people kept you and the grave clothes they made for you and live indeed amongst the living. You may have lost blood, but should you lose your humanity? Come forth!!! Lose the hurt and the pain, lose everything that is hindering blood from flowing, and embrace a new life and world of unrestricted possibilities. Yes, you may have been to the land of the dead, but you've been called forth because you still have more life to live, enjoy, and lives to impact. You can't be numb any further; you can't turn a blind eye any further; it's time to step out and step up. If you remain numb you are simply choosing to be dead to life, and what fellowship has death and life?

You need to trust again; you need to love again, and you need to do those things you swore not to do again because you were hurt... I know you miss them and I can tell you that every single day you remain numb you miss much more the life of life, but if you will take in oxygen and allow blood to flow in you again and tell the hurt you'll not be buried alive, you will be amazed what you can offer life now that you've been through the deadly situation and back. Can I welcome you back? Of course, Yes!!

Welcome back!!!

You can live again truly and full of blood, and much life.... You don't need to live with them, but don't allow what they did to bury you; I pray you see the life that forgiveness can give.

THE COLD-PEOPLE:

One of the ways to know that something is dead is when it stops being warm and starts getting so cold. The cold people are people who have let their dreams die, those who have let those

POUR

childhood fantasies vanish, and strangled the life of their passion. They are at work but have no zeal; they are in the group bodily but mentally detached; they are in the marriage but mentally separated; they are in the game but mentally exhausted; they are in the fight but mentally defeated. Hurt and unforgiveness can get you to the place where you are cold towards everything and everyone that once meant something to you.

Unlike the no-blood people, you are available, but you come cold; you welcome people into your life, but they meet you cold. Have you ever been served a cold meal in winter? It is not that the food was not well decorated; only that it was served cold. When hurt and memories make you cold, you are losing life!

No wonder your zeal is punctured; no wonder you easily get irritated and choose to stay alone in the dark.

It is time for you to love life again, stay, and rub your minds with nature and the beautiful things that mean a lot to you. Something has got to fan up your flame but you got to stay close to people and things that can spark the fire back in you. How did you let that warmth go out of your life that much, except that you focused on what broke you so much that you allowed brokenness to become the tool the enemy used to cover your light? Can't you see that what you focused on has defined your lifestyle?

Well, I came with my fists clinched on the defibrillator to preach forgiveness to you. You can choose to get your light back and love again; you can fight again, you can support again, you can walk again, you can preach again, and you can even start all over again. Don't let what you've been through because the right people chose to do the wrong things to you stop you from getting out of their mess and living your life in Victory. It is time to get out of the cold places of life and turn to God to give you light.

Forgiveness is what you owe them for your sake. You can turn a broken system into an edifice if you climb over the hurt and disappointments and hand down forgiveness to those who have hurt you so badly. They could have won ultimately and knocked you out of life if you chose to hold on to the past and refuse to move on.

You can heal from anything if you choose to; you can come out of anything if you choose to. If you survived then and even without blood flowing within, you got the opportunity to read this chapter; it means there is hope for you to live again with so much vigor.

Holding on without forgiveness has made your life turn out cold, you have begun to see life from the lenses of your hurt and this is why you are feeling bitter, but I call you out of bitterness and sadness into God's marvelous light, and like our savior who despite hanging on the cross for what he didn't do, went to his grave without a grudge, we know how after three days he resurrected in glory and is now sitting at the right hand of the father having all things under his feet. I charge you to give forgiveness a chance and see how God's supernatural healing flows into your life to bring you back alive and well.

It is time to experience a new life, I want you to take this second chance and make the best out of it.

I love you and I want to see you win!!

POUR

OVERCOMING REJECTION

"And when they came nigh to Jerusalem, unto Bethphage and Bethany, at the mount of Olives, he sendeth forth two of his disciples, And saith unto them, Go your way into the village over against you: and as soon as ye be entered into it, ye shall find a colt tied, whereon never man sat; lose him, and bring him.

And if any man say unto you, Why do ye this? Say ye that the Lord hath need of him; and straightway he will send him hither."

-- Mark 11:1-3 KJV.

This is about a donkey (colt) that was tied up in Bethphage near Bethany. Bethphage is a village in Israel; it is located about three miles away from the entrance of the great city gates of Jerusalem. The village of Bethphage on Mount Olives was one of the most important centers for the Judahite authorities in the period of the Messiah and the Apostles. There were specific decisions of the Sanhedrin that were reserved for determination only at this official seat of the court in Bethphage. Those were decisions affecting what were the limits of the camp of Israel around the city of Jerusalem.

The reason that this type of decision was to be made at this special village on the east side of Jerusalem is because it is at the 'entrance' to Jerusalem. There are Biblical implications for that; we may not go into that for now, but just so you know, Jerusalem was the capital city of the nation, and the principal gate to the city was on the eastern side close to Bethphage. By the way, the word "Bethphage" means the House of unripe figs.

As Jesus prepared for his triumphant entry into Jerusalem, guess the vessel he chose to use; that colt that was tied up, probably rejected and thought was useless for no one has ever ridden on it. The colt was tied up at the entrance of the village. Jesus may have taken note of that colt since the days of his visit to Bethany to see his friends Lazarus, Mary, and Martha, or got to know that the colt was tied up there by revelation. In this story, we find Jesus' triumphant entry preparation, we find the colt that was tied up, and we find the people who would ask why anyone would think of untying the colt; we also discover that this colt was tied up because it is considered unworthy to be ridden. Jesus saw the potential in the colt that those who tied it didn't see.

LaTonia Harrell

Rejection comes in different directions, from people in one direction, and from ourselves in another direction. When rejection comes from within a person, it is self-inflicted: that person will not be able to see his or her worth. Sometimes, the effect of experiencing a series of rejections from other people enforces rejection from ourselves. You can deal with people rejecting you, but how can you deal with you rejecting you?

Many times limitations in our lives come from the feelings of diverse kinds of rejections. I carefully chose to use the word "feelings," because it is a feeling. It may not have the impact it poses unless you allow it to become your perspective or conviction. Many times, we see in scripture that the rejected stone became the chief cornerstone, and that's because the rejected stone didn't conclude that it was not useful. After all, others couldn't see its worth. I want to tell you that your worth is not in your demand; your worth is in your purpose. Joseph faced criticism and hate from the closest people in his life, yet he never hated himself; he went through betrayal and was framed, but he was still relevant in prison. Your purpose is what should give you a sense of your worth, not necessarily your demand because there are times your demand will drop, but your purpose never drops.

The donkey in our text was tied up only three miles away from where it was going to be celebrated. A moment later, people were taking off their clothes, cutting off branches of palms, and laying them down for the donkey to walk on because of who she was carrying. I dare say that that donkey was carrying purpose on her back! Immediately, she availed herself to carry purpose; those who questioned why she was being untied had a purposeful response, "The master needs it". There is a difference between wanting something and needing something, anyone who needs something is mandated to do anything possible to get it. Imagine how the donkey is going to feel that evening and eventually after the triumphant entry, "I drove a king."

While the scriptures are silent about why the colt was tied up in the first place, the scripture is not silent about how the master needs it.

Nothing unties someone from the feelings of rejection like a sense of purpose! You can cry about being rejected, you can cry about not being counted in, you can cry about not getting the attention you need, but the day you wipe those tears and take on your assignment on purpose, you will move from being rejected to being needed. What I see a lot of people do is that they want to feel accepted by those who rejected them, friends, chances are slim that that might happen; they want to feel compensated. They want the testimony to sound thus: Four years ago, I was rejected by Pastor Latonia, and three months later, she came begging that she needed me back. You see, a testimony like this can massage our ego but that's the reason a lot of people are yoked to a dysfunction, they are even tied to a chair they can carry to a welder to cut off the

POUR

chains but they won't because their ego tells them that "they'll come back for me." They are bent on proving a point rather than moving forward. There is no guarantee that those who dropped you off will come back to pick you up, (why would you even want them to come back and meet you where they left you?), There is no guarantee that those who rejected you will be the same people to discern your worth; there is no guarantee for that. What you should focus on is being available to those who have discerned your worth and get on with your life. The distance between where you were rejected and where you are now being celebrated can even be three miles away, what's important is that you are not where you used to be.

The master's need of you is your chance to be untied. Notice again from the text that those who tied the colt are different from those who untied the colt. Being rejected is not the end of your life; there is a good chance that you can be celebrated even three miles away from where you used to be. The question is this: when those who will untie you from that limitation come with a sense of urgency and purpose, will you go with them into the city gates, forgetting about your chains and the scars the chains imprinted, or would you stay for revenge or prove your relevance to them?

Some points you fight to prove may not be more necessary than moving on.

I believe these words are coming to you at this point in your life because your kings are coming to the brightness of your light. Though tied, Jesus needed the colt. I'd like to share a few strategies that will help you overcome rejection and the pain of rejection.

1. YOUR REVENGE IS GROWTH.

Growth Hurts but it is profitable!

You cannot fulfill destiny if you are not willing to grow.

Sometimes, certain rejection forces us to grow; it forces us to look within. Negative feedback can force you to push boundaries if you let it, you can choose to be inspired or intimidated. Certain values come to you naturally because you grew up, and certain possibilities happen with you not because you went to a new place but because you outgrew your former self. Your development is a statement of value and productivity, and instead of feeling sorry for yourself or the rejection you faced, allow yourself to evolve. You'll have to reintroduce yourself to even people who conspired against you, like in the case of Joseph. How come his brothers didn't recognize him? His life had transformed because he dreamed more even when it attracted more hate. There are areas of your life that become greater because you used your rejection as fuel to inspire greatness within you.

2. DON'T CRACK YOUR CHARACTER

Some rejections are a test of time; they are a test of character. When you want to know if someone is truly committed to a thing for his or her gain, temporally cut off some benefits, act like you don't need them, and watch what comes out next. If they are real with you, they'll respectfully appeal, but if they are just about the position or showing off some fake loyalty, their attitude will change. Growth builds your patience, but also it builds your character. As long as your character is refined through what you are going through, you stand a chance to be a better version of yourself. This means that instead of getting bitter, you get better.

3. NEVER MAKE IT ABOUT YOURSELF.

Everyone at different points in their lives goes through different phases of rejection. If you understand that rejection is not about yourself you can handle rejection without getting sentimentally attached to it. Many people don't get this right: as such, they start talking down on themselves; they start thinking maybe something about them is not right or maybe they didn't do a thing right. When you begin to talk to yourself without Honor or from a broken state, you become vulnerable to what happened to you and start distorting what can happen to you. You need to learn that what sinks a ship is not the intensity of the storm around it; it is the leakages in the boat that sinks the ship. When you beat yourself too hard you start puncturing systems that were in place to secure you even in turbulent times.

Deal with rejection as rejection; don't make it about yourself, something you did, or something you didn't do. If you were rejected today, you can be accepted tomorrow. If they reject you, another person will accept you. It's that simple.

4. EMBRACE SELF LOVE.

You can be hated for doing the right thing as well as when you do the wrong things. This is why I told you not to make a rejection of yourself. You handle rejection better when you still go down and honor yourself while going down. You cannot stop being kind to yourself, or taking care of yourself because you were rejected, no!

POUR

This is one of the times to remind yourself that you are coming out of this and you will be where you desire to be. If it is yet to manifest, it will someday and you are not willing to manipulate your way to get into positions you know are destined to be for you.

It is self-love that enables you to see yourself correctly from the lenses of love and celebrate your disappointing situation with grace, knowing that this, too, shall pass.

Adequate self-love enables you to come out of anything, even with the right attitude. Yes, your proposal was rejected. Write to someone else, apply somewhere else, develop other skills, and grow in other areas.

Rejection is not a dead end. It has been proven many times to be a pathway to greater glory. They say that when one door closes, another one opens. You have to ensure that you don't allow the impact of not getting what you want, or being hindered from what you deserve to stop you from preparing yourself to walk into another open door. Remember, those who tied the colt are different from those who loosed it.

LaTonia Harrell

TRANSFORMING BROKENNESS INTO STRENGTH

If you look carefully, you will find that there is a purpose in pain. You can turn pressure to power. Those who find the strength to carry on are those who have learned to look at the reflection in the mirror with grace. There are three ways to get delivered from a situation: it is either God takes it out of you, or He takes you out of it, or He takes you through it until you come out of it. Whichever way He chooses to deliver you understand that He does it with the intention that it serves a better purpose. Many times people have wondered why the love of God will still allow one to go through an unpleasant situation, what they do not know is that there are unpleasant situations that build a person's character more than lovey-dovey would. The essence of the law was to bring man to the end of himself. The essence of fellowship is to reach out to each other according to our measures of grace. This grace is cultivated through moments of despair, just like forgiveness is cultivated through moments of hurt, pain, and betrayal. Likewise, strength is built in moments of brokenness.

"And the Lord said, Simon, Simon, behold, Satan hath desired to have you, that he may sift you as wheat: But I have prayed for thee, that thy faith fail not: and when thou art converted, strengthen thy brethren." Luke 22:31-32

Satan had desired to sift Peter because of the fear in his heart; more so, there was doubt in his heart which fear had produced, and there was Satan who saw it as an opportunity to break Peter and his brothers. If Peter had fallen, perhaps the rest would have fallen without recovery. Jesus saw it coming, and he prayed for Peter and asked him to strengthen his brothers when he had fully recovered. Many ministries are lost not because the ministers are not powerful or effective or yielded; it is because the Grace to impart cannot come from a vessel that is bleeding. You have to recover fully to impart certain levels of grace and health. You have to recover from hurt to help another heal from theirs. Part of the process of helping other people get healing is that you have to get your strength back to be able to strengthen others. Forgiveness is what you give; it is the price you pay to gain back your strength; it is the price you pay to come alive again. You must have bled, you may have gone numb at some point, but for you to live again and restore healing to the rest of the world that needs it, especially your brethren, you have to forgive.

POUR

There is strength in forgiveness; it is the kind of strength that looks at the scars and instead of feeling pained, you are inspired by it because it is a sign that you recovered. Yes, you have to live with the scars for the rest of your life, but thank God you don't have to live with the pain or the grudge for the rest of your life. When you look at the scars, what does it remind you of, healing or pain?

Let me spend some time speaking to those who have been through something that broke them so bad that it left a scar at the most important part of their lives.

The truth is that you cannot change the scar, but you can change how you look at it; you cannot change what has happened, but you can transform it with a better narrative. The story doesn't have to end with your scar, it can end with the purpose you give to the scar; maybe because you went through it like Peter, you can have the capacity to strengthen those going through it, or you can become the precaution sign that other millions have to read not to go in the direction you went already, either way, your scar will be doing more good than damage.

Jesus Christ had scars, but by his stripes, billions of us are healed. Thomas pierced his hands through the scars on his palm and that further strengthened the conviction of his salvation.

BEYOND THE SCARS

Let me share a few moments with you on this that could spark up hope and even though you may still have some scars, you can still recover. This is from a friend to another friend. We may not have gone through the same degree of pain, but one thing we have in common is the scars, and it is going to be there with us for a long time, probably forever.

To some people, the scars remind them of the injury and all they had to go through, what they had to give up, the degree of pain they had to endure, and what life was like before the incident(s).

But can I show you another perspective on it?

Right then, look at it this way: The scars should remind you of your ability to heal --- beyond the scars, there is healing, there is the opportunity to move on or start over, the opportunity to give another shot; there is a testimony of not being knocked out!! So many people are locked up in the closets of unforgiveness because when they look at their scars, it reminds them of how the scars came about, and as such, they burst into tears, feeling depressed, angry, desolated, used, victimized, or dumped, but this should not be your response because you now know better. You may have had it rough in the past or maybe having it rough now but you sure have moved on since you can call it "yesterday" or "a few hours ago", you have to be strong enough to separate yourself from the past and be present in the future--- the past has always had a 'stronghold' on people who wouldn't let it go.

You are different; you are brave to see the brighter side of life. Sometimes God allows us to go through certain things and allows them to happen to us so that we can teach other people how to be strong and courageous, how to face challenging times and be brave enough to conquer them. You may now have lived with the scars, but don't forget that beyond the scars is a courageous victory; beyond the scars is a star that fought its way through the dark moments to shine; beyond the scars is someone who endured a series of pain, fights to hold back tears, and finally succeeded.

Blessed of it all is that beyond the scars is a greater, bigger, brighter, and better you. Whenever treasures go through the fires (heat), they shine brighter, and their value increase. God has a great plan for you, be strong.

"But it was the Lord's good plan to crush Him and cause Him grief, yet when his life is made an offering for Sin, he will have many descendants. He will enjoy a long life, and the Lord's good plans will prosper in His hands". Isaiah 53:10.

Sarah was barren, and Haggai laughed at her. Every day, it broke her heart and wounded her spirit, but if only she knew that her son would signify the promise: the seed of Abraham. Little did she know she would give birth to Isaac and become the mother of many nations. She can be bitter that she was barren for those number of years or thank God that she is preserved by favor to give birth to Isaac the father of Israel. Sometimes, what we go through is not just for us but for others who are coming out after us; this is why we need to be careful about how we respond to even things we cannot understand and trust God in the process. Your challenge may be historical or figurative or a breakthrough that liberates not just you but millions of people around the world. This is why you need courage and strength!

THE LARGE HEART

Forgiveness allows you to develop a large heart; you would have deeper empathy, your sympathy won't be a cliché, and your concern and care will be true because you have gone through something that gave you perspective about what other people may be dealing with. Now, in your leadership techniques, there is no marginalization. There is equity because you have sat where others sit and understand better. Your heart is right and pure towards everything you do because

POUR

certain pains have circumcised your heart and purified it, you can see what is not obvious and hear what is not said. This makes your life more of a blessing than it could have been if you had a clean slate.

Pain connected you with purpose and even though what you went through was painful, you have allowed it to preach a Gospel that is only embodied through pain. This is the strength that Jesus told Peter about, "When you are converted, strengthen your brethren."

DRINK THE CUP

The price of forgiveness is to see and focus on a greater purpose than what you have to go through to become.

"And he was withdrawn from them about a stone's cast, and kneeled down, and prayed, Saying, Father, if thou be willing, remove this cup from me: nevertheless not my will, but thine, be done." Luke 22:41-42

Listen, friends, forgiveness is painful and is not always easy. Even Jesus prayed through one of the most difficult seasons of his lifetime on earth. The season where he was going to embody forgiveness. The will of the Father Is that we drink the cup!

I pray that you receive grace to drink the cup even though naturally it is uncomfortable to drink the cup; understand that your harvest will be more, and your reward will be greater.

As we forgive those who trespass against us, may the Glory of the Lord prevail in our lives.

HEALING OVER BETRAYAL

I put this piece together for you to have an opportunity to imagine what Judas' side of the story could have been. Betrayal comes mostly from people we trust and who are close to us; otherwise, it wouldn't be called betrayal. People betray people for so many reasons and one of the most common is for selfish reasons.

JUDAS' SIDE OF THE STORY

"The whole thing started exactly two days before the Passover. We were in the house of Simon the leper when a woman came to see Jesus (you know how careful we disciples are about women coming to Jesus). This one even came with a very expensive perfume, ah, Alabaster box!!

That was my first time seeing it.

Only a few people in Israel have an Alabaster box; it is very, very expensive.

To be honest, I was not the one who said we could have sold it and used the money or given it to the poor. It was Peter, who said something like that first, and everybody started saying the same thing; we were angry, and I don't know who told Jesus that that was how we felt about someone pouring oil perfume on his legs.

Jesus started telling us that she was preparing him for the crucifixion.

Even up till now, people think I am the one who said that Jesus should have sold the perfume because I was the one managing the account and also in charge of buying anything that we needed.

POUR

Later, as I was going out she and I met the chiefs outside, along with the scribes and Pharisees. I was very angry about how they almost turned everything on me as if I was the only one who said we could have sold the oil; I didn't even say it. They said it, but all eyes were on me when JESUS started asking why we were angry and insisting that we sell the perfume or give the money from selling it to the poor. What it was annoyed me more was when he said one of us would betray him, and Peter started asking who; he was looking at me in some way while he was asking Jesus.

Okay, when I went outside to cool off as I said earlier, I saw People gathered, and it was the scribes and Pharisees; I went there. I knew it was because of Jesus that they gathered there, and it was because of them that we came inside. When I met one of the chiefs outside, I asked him what they'd give me if I gave them JESUS our master... Honestly, I didn't know that Jesus would even allow them to capture him; I didn't know that they'd kill him.

They told me that they'd give me 30 pieces of silver. I said okay and I left. I didn't even meet them again.

Two days later, it was the day of the Passover: everything was fine and we were happy for the day of Passover. It was the first day; Peter suggested that we should go and find out where Jesus would like to have his own Passover celebration ahead of the evening.

We all went to ask Jesus as Peter suggested, He told us where he prefers. We went straight away and secured the venue (it was the house of one brother); in the evening, after we finished eating and praying as usual, Jesus even washed our feet.

As he was talking about the same thing he talked about two days ago, I didn't know what came over me and eventually entered me.

First, I felt as though they were accusing me of something, and my mind was telling me to go on and just do it and let it end there.

John 13:2

"And supper being ended, the devil having now put into the heart of Judas Iscariot, Simon's son, to betray him;"

When Jesus told me that I should go and do what was in my mind, I thought it was part of the plan, you know what Jesus used to do? Most times, people want to catch him and how he will get home before we do. Sometimes, it makes me feel like he disappeared. I thought that's what he'll do that night.

Immediately, he told me to go on with what was on my mind, and that was when I left to meet with the chiefs, who told me they wanted to apprehend him. Honestly, I don't know what entered me and made me so bold.

John 13:2, 27

[2]And supper being ended, the devil having now put into the heart of Judas Iscariot, Simon's son, to betray him;

[27]And after the sop Satan entered into him. Then said Jesus unto him, That thou doest, do quickly.

Even the disciples thought I went to buy something. Truly, it is not as bad as People make it look; where it got bad was when I saw how they arrested JESUS and started beating him.

John 13:29

[29]Some of them thought that because Judas had the bag, Jesus had said unto him, Buy those things that we need against the feast, or that he should give something to the poor.

The way he looked at me as one who was helpless, then I knew I had sold him out. I'm sorry"

What if this story was truly Judas' story?

It shows us that the people that betray people do have a great reason but it is usually a selfish reason. Like Judas, perhaps he thought Jesus would save himself, on the other hand, God planned to deliver Jesus to the chiefs to start the redemption project. Joseph was betrayed by his brothers because they hated him yet God used their plot against him to fulfill his plan for Israel.

POUR

Could it be that we can discern the purpose of betrayal if we are walking in the purpose of God? As hurtful as it can be, it is still one of the tools God uses to push us into destiny. When you do your best to be kind to people, when you do your best to love people sincerely, yet they betray you, understand that if you are in the will of God, He got you. You can start looking at it differently, like Jesus, when he was on the cross, cried out to God to forgive them, and Joseph looked at his brothers and told them what the devil meant for evil; God turned it for their good. Betrayal will always hurt deeper when you are still at the level you were betrayed, even after several years. Do you know that you can be betrayed and yet get better?

Yes, you can get better as soon as you look beyond it and press for the will and purpose of God to be fulfilled.

I say this to help you understand that whatever you put under purpose shines brighter because purpose empowers it: I've spoken to a lot of people who have been hurt in so many areas of their lives, martially, relationally, and otherwise, and I keep telling them that it is a personal decision by the help of God to heal from anything.

Any hurt you won't present to the healer won't heal.

You can't hold onto any grudge and expect healing. It's painful but Jesus Christ is greater! Let him touch your heart friend, you'll be fine!

Healing is a Supernatural flow of God into a situation. Desiring to be healed means you want to get better and well; it means that you have been bashed in some way, but you want to be healed. People don't go to the hospital to explain how sad they are about what happened to them, they go there because they want to be free from pain and resentment. This is what happens when you surrender your hurt and let go of the people that hurt you. You start healing faster when you focus on healing as your chance to live a greater life. Nothing holds back the Grace to be healed like the grudge in the heart; a grudge is toxic to the peaceful process of healing. You may desire to be healed, but if you do not purge yourself of any grudge, anger, or malice, the process will take longer or never happen. Forgiveness is for your good; healing is for your good, and deliverance is for your good. If you love yourself truly which I believe you do and appreciate that you do, you will not hold back any one of those from yourself.

Rehearsing the hurt won't make it go; it will rather make the pain go deeper, but renewing your mind to the possibility of a better, rewarding life with the purifications of healing will uplift you and keep you in perfect peace.

The good news is that you can heal from anything if you so desire. The first step is to see the big picture; purpose!

I've been hurt, but I've got a purpose for my life; I can live life blessing others with my experience gained because I healed from my betrayal. Anyone can betray someone but only you can decide to heal from anything.

I invite you, therefore, to see the advantage of healing and give yourself a chance to live without hurt or grudge.

I leave you with these words:

Jesus can fix your brokenness if you hand it over to him. Take a deep breath and just let it go all in his hands.

It will amaze you who you can become when he is done with you.

POUR

SELF-CARE

In the sequel to the last chapter on healing over betrayal, I will be sharing insights to enable you to build trust in yourself and rebuild trust in others. A lot of people take care of other people's business while neglecting theirs, and this does not make you selfless; it makes you hypocritical because the rule says to love others as you love yourself. This means that I can't give what I can't have and you don't give what you can't have. Many people take time to care for other people, but they end up feeling guilty when they extend the same measure of love to themselves. I think something is wrong with that!

Part of the communication of your value system stems from how you treat yourself; in fact, nobody will treat you better than you treat yourself because in treating yourself, in valuing yourself, in giving yourself first place, you show others how to deal with you. They can trust how you deal with them by watching how you deal with yourself; if you are having a hard time caring for yourself or giving yourself valuable things, people have a hard time receiving valuable things from you. When they say charity begins at home, you are your home; you've got to Honor yourself as much as you Honor other people.

How well do you honor yourself?

In case you are having a hard time spending time with yourself or giving yourself what you deserve, here are a few things to help you understand:

Self-care entails that you are paying adequate attention to your body, your soul, and your spirit. It is not one only at the expense of the other. Let's go a little further on this.

As I stated in the previous chapter, man is tripartite, having the body, soul, and spirit. The body represents the physical gateway, the soul represents the mental or intellectual gateway, and the spirit represents the spiritual gateway. By this simple narrative, we understand that what gets to the body can be through our skin, eyes, ears, nose, and mouth. What gets to the mind is through our consciousness or self-consciousness, and what gets to our spirit is through the Holy Spirit. This way, we understand that man has physical, mental, and spiritual capacity. In all, we see that our body, soul, and spirit are involved in our service to God and humanity. These components make up the total individual.

Your body is a physical tool that houses your soul and spirit. Immediately life leaves the body, the soul and the spirit can no longer have access to the tangible world. However, as much as the body is a physical and complete entity, it cannot function without a command from the mind where the soul resides. Our body also reflects our physical health. Longevity is a promise to the body, not to the soul or spirit; if we do not take care of our bodies, our bodies will fall ill and cut short the purposes of God in our lives. What we eat and what we drink affects our physical health directly. Therefore, it is wise to choose our diet profitably to sustain life in the body. It is important to eat healthy meals, regularly exercise the body, and keep a clean environment. Avoid violence, going to places, or doing things that can endanger your life or deform any part of your body due to sustained injury. For instance, over-speeding, texting while driving, or going swimming without a life jacket can endanger your life.

"For bodily exercise profiteth little: but godliness is profitable unto all things, having promise of the life that now is, and of that which is to come." 1 Timothy 4:8 KJV

"And God said, Behold, I have given you every herb bearing seed, which is upon the face of all the earth, and every tree, in the which is the fruit of a tree yielding seed; to you, it shall be for meat." Genesis 1:29 KJV

Your mind is where your consciousness and subconscious activities take place. It holds your emotions, your memories, and your desires. It is in your mind that hope, esteem, success, or failure is stored. Whatever you see or hear or feel gets stored in your mind. Information is processed and stored in your mind. The body and the spirit supply the mind with content to carry out whatever it will later instruct the body to execute. The mind, which is your soul, is the middle ground and is never a vacuum. This means that our minds are never empty. We are either meditating on a scene from a movie we watched yesterday or we are meditating on what our loved one said on our way back from work, or we are meditating on the scripture we read before we slept last night.

If the spirit does not regulate the activities of the mind, ensuring that our soul is regenerated, our mind or soul will lead our bodies to sin. There is such a thing as the Salvation of the soul and it is through the working of the spirit. Whatever enters and stays in the soul determines the course of the man's destiny, morals, principles, and beliefs. It also has a way of setting his strength or weakness.

POUR

" For as he thinketh in his heart, so is he: Eat and drink, saith he to thee; but his heart is not with thee." Proverbs 23:7.

Your intellectual capacity, your strength, is a function of what you feed your mind daily. What sustains your mental capacity is the richness of what you allow to get to your mind. Remember, how you respond in the form of emotions, wisdom or knowledge depends on the health of your mind.

Your spirit is the safest place on Earth because it is where God lives. This is where the true and authentic impact or will of God for a man or in a man resides. Your spirit is the candle of the Lord.

"The spirit of man is the candle of the LORD, searching all the inward parts of the belly." Proverbs 20:27 KJV. Most of God's promises and all of God's word are stored in our spirit: the Salvation of the soul never happens outside the impact of the spirit; the Holy Ghost works with our spirit to educate the mind. This education is called the renewal of the mind. As we understood a while ago that the mind could receive information from our spirit, it is important to note that whenever the spirit is in control of the activities of the mind, we experience life and Peace. Whatever you will receive from the Spirit of God must be received through your spirit and then sent to your mind or soul for it to manifest physically in your life. To the degree that the soul receives from the spirit that's the degree to which the individual is transformed. Transformation happens in the mind; you must ensure that your mind is not interrupting the fellowship of your spirit with the Spirit of God.

"The spirit of a man will sustain his infirmity; but a wounded spirit who can bear?" Proverbs 18:14.

Self-care goes beyond buying yourself groceries, taking yourself out, or having some quiet time; it provides the responsibility for you to take care of your body, soul, and spirit. Ensuring that none of these entities are poorly treated or casually equipped. When you ensure the holistic health and development of your body, soul, and spirit and have mastered how to care for each of them, you are expressing authority, dominion, and influence. To the degree that you have control of what happens within you, that is the degree that you are going to have control over what happens around you.

I desire that you begin to see how much God loves you and that he entrusts the responsibility of developing yourself to you. Now you know that this is not just about only how you feel but the overall fullness of who you are. You are the steward of your body, soul, and spirit, are you faithful in taking care of yourself?

THE POWER OF PRAYER

"And I sought for a man among them, that should make up the hedge, and stand in the gap before me for the land, that I should not destroy it: but I found none." Ezekiel 22:30

There is extreme power in prayer!

Prayer is the lifeline of operation in the kingdom of God. Many times we see in scripture that God expects us to pray.

"And he spake a parable unto them to this end, that men ought always to pray, and not to faint;" Luke 18:1. Man was not wired to go through life all by himself: He is the creation of God, and as such God is responsible for him.

What exactly does it mean to pray and why must we pray?

PRAYER IS A BOND:

God desires a relationship with mankind and of all his creation, man is the creature he chose to have a personal relationship with. God is love and he is relational: After the fall of man, God had to send his Son to die instead of man to redeem the relationship he had with man from the beginning.

So God created man in his own image, in the image of God created he him; male and female created he them.

    Genesis 1:27 KJV

Man was created in the image and likeness of God, Man the tendency to be relational. Even though man fell through disobedience, God didn't leave man without help or restoration. Jesus Christ came as the second Adam to fulfill the law because through Adam death and Sin reigned but through Jesus Christ there is redemption: "For as by one man's disobedience many were made sinners, so by the obedience of one shall many be made righteous. Moreover the law entered, that the offence might abound. But where sin abounded, grace did much more abound: That as sin hath reigned unto death, even so might grace reign through righteousness unto eternal life by Jesus Christ our Lord." Romans 5:19-20.

This was how Man was to be redeemed back to life: "For God so loved the world, that he gave his only begotten Son, that whosoever believeth in him should not perish, but have everlasting life." John 3:16.

Life in Christ and through Jesus Christ became the only way to have and maintain a relationship with God. As the Scripture tells us about Christ: "In whom we have redemption through his blood, even the forgiveness of sins: Who is the image of the invisible God, the firstborn of every creature: For by him were all things created, that are in heaven, and that are in earth, visible and invisible, whether they be thrones, or dominions, or principalities, or powers: all things were created by him, and for him:" Colossians 1:14-16.

The man Jesus Christ became our high priest and the mediator between God and man. God deals with Jesus Christ on behalf of Man and Man deals with Jesus Christ as the way to the Father.

I had to explain all these to show you the relationship between God the Father and His son Jesus Christ and then our relationship with Jesus Christ. God is more concerned about our relationship with him and this is why he'd sacrifice his son to get us back. Such mystery!

Prayer becomes a bond because it is a way of communication for lovers only. When we pray we are addressing God directly as Father through our loyalty or relationship with his Son. The reason Jesus Christ is the Way to the Father's heart is because He pleased the Father in the exact area Adam displeased the Father. Amazing isn't it?

This is why when the disciples told Jesus Christ to teach them to pray, he rather taught them how to pray:

"And it came to pass, that, as he was praying in a certain place, when he ceased, one of his disciples said unto him, Lord, teach us to pray, as John also taught his disciples. And he said unto them, When ye pray, say, Our Father which art in heaven, Hallowed be thy name. Thy kingdom come. Thy will be done, as in heaven, so in earth." Luke 11:1-2 KJV.

POUR

Jesus by extension taught us the model of prayer. He recognized that there is a relationship that connects us to the Father, wherefore we can cry out to him "My Daddy", we can call him Father because He gave birth to us by his Spirit.

This is one of the first things you must know whenever you go to God in prayer, He is your Father!

You have a relationship with him through the blood of Jesus Christ and you have access to him as his Son or Daughter.

PRAYER IS LEGISLATIVE:

When we pray, we enforce the will of God on earth as it is in Heaven. The will of God is his purpose for man on earth and his intentions for activities on earth through man and other beings on earth. Man was given absolute dominion over things on earth and God can trust man to enforce his will on earth because man has the Spirit of God. Prayer is the way to announce the purposes of God on earth or to make it a decree on earth through levels of spiritual intelligence and spiritual maturity.

Man has a delegated authority to act instead of God on earth. So that whatever you bind on earth is bound in heaven and whatever you loose on earth is loosed in heaven.

This is why you shall decree a thing on earth and it is established: you have been given authority to enforce the will of God on earth.

This is why there are different kinds of prayers and they all function through different levels of legislation.

PRAYER IS INTIMACY

Due to the relationship between God and man through Christ Jesus, prayer becomes a powerful force of intimacy. God reveals his heart to the spirit of the man as he communes with God through prayer.

"Likewise the Spirit also helpeth our infirmities: for we know not what we should pray for as we ought: but the Spirit itself maketh intercession for us with groanings which cannot be uttered." Romans 8:26

The Spirit to spirit connection enables us to fellowship with God and also have privy to his desires and will.

"I beseech you therefore, brethren, by the mercies of God, that ye present your bodies a living sacrifice, holy, acceptable unto God, which is your reasonable service. And be not conformed to this world: but be ye transformed by the renewing of your mind, that ye may prove what is that good, and acceptable, and perfect, will of God." Romans 12:1-2.

You remember our last conversation about the communication between the soul, spirit and body? It is helpful in this context: when we renew our minds by the information supplied to our minds by the Spirit of God, we are able to prove what the Will of God is, his perfect will.

It is during these sessions of prayer that God reveals his will to us about a situation or his desires in our lives.

PRAYER IS HUMILITY:

"If my people, which are called by my name, shall humble themselves, and pray, and seek my face, and turn from their wicked ways; then will I hear from heaven, and will forgive their sin, and will heal their land." 2 Chronicles 7:14

Praying is a sign of surrender and humility to God. It shows that you acknowledge that God is omniscient, Omnipotent, and Omnipresent. He is almighty and can help you get to whatever you want as a child rely on his parents for survival. When you pray you are asking, seeking and knocking doors only God your father can open.

POUR

When we pray, we are simply allowing ourselves to be vulnerable with Our Father, we are able to share our deepest desires with him knowing that he cares but first, our heart must be focused on him as the only way!

Let me show you a method:

"Humble yourselves therefore under the mighty hand of God, that he may exalt you in due time:" 1 Peter 5:6

How do you get God to lift you up?

The answer is in verse 7,

"Casting all your care upon him; for he careth for you." 1 Peter 5:7 KJV.

When we humble ourselves and surrender ourselves to God as incapable, he lifts us up in due season, and we do so by casting our care upon him. Anytime you worry about your bills, your children, your husband, your paycheck, or your project it is because you are not casting it on him. And that is perceived as Pride!

You don't own yourself; you are not by yourself, besides you are created to depend on your Father God for everything. This is why he is your Father!

The power of prayer therefore is exerted whenever you come to the end of yourself and totally depend on the one who is all powerful, all knowing and can get into anywhere without a barrier. It is acknowledging that you have a relationship advantage with the Almighty God who is lavishly in love with you and mindful of you.

The power of prayer is in your humility to acknowledge God as your father and go ahead to tell him what you need in faith!

LaTonia Harrell

"Be careful for nothing; but in everything by prayer and supplication with thanksgiving let your requests be made known unto God. And the peace of God, which passeth all understanding, shall keep your hearts and minds through Christ Jesus." Philippians 4:6-7 KJV.

POUR

A Prayer for Those Who Feel They Have No Purpose

Heavenly Father, we lift up those who feel lost and without direction. May they find clarity and understanding in their lives, discovering the unique purpose you have for them. Surround them with your love and guidance, and help them see the value they bring to the world. In Jesus Christ's mighty name, we pray, amen.

A Prayer for Men Ready to Take a Stand and Walk in Their Purpose

Lord, we pray for the men who are seeking to embrace their true calling. Grant them the courage to stand firm in their convictions and the wisdom to pursue their purpose with passion. Empower them to be leaders and examples in their communities, reflecting your strength and love. In Jesus Christ's mighty name, we pray, amen.

A Prayer for Women to Walk in Their Purpose

Dear God, we ask for your blessings upon the women striving to fulfill their divine purpose. Help them to embrace their gifts and talents, and guide them as they navigate their paths. May they find strength in their identity and inspire others along the way. In Jesus Christ's mighty name, we pray, amen.

A Prayer for Those Trying to Forgive and Move On

Heavenly Father, we seek your grace for those struggling to forgive and let go of past hurts. Help them to find healing in their hearts and the strength to release any bitterness. May they experience the freedom that comes from forgiveness and find peace in moving forward. In Jesus Christ's mighty name, we pray, amen.

A Prayer for Strength to Move Forward

Lord, we ask for your strength for those facing challenges and uncertainties. Grant them the resilience to overcome obstacles and the faith to trust in your plan. Help them to take each step with confidence and hope, knowing that you are always with them. In Jesus Christ's mighty name, we pray, amen.

www.ingramcontent.com/pod-product-compliance
Lightning Source LLC
Chambersburg PA
CBHW071230160426
43196CB00012B/2473